Contents

Chapter 1 – Setting the Scene

For nearly 20 years, I have operated in and around the talent universe as someone who has hired people, fired people and helped other people literally hire hundreds of others. I think it's fair to say that I have seen the good, the bad and the downright ugly in the field. Don't even for a minute think that global professional service firms or blue-chip companies are a paragon of virtue when compared to struggling start-ups. I have found that organisations – both large and small – have some excellent as well as diabolical processes. Even more shocking is the millions that firms waste on obtaining talent through inefficient process, over-complicated interview schedules and duplication.

Cheaper than recruiting people is retaining people, and retention starts at recruitment. Recruitment is the start of your new employee's journey with you. It sets the initial tone of the relationship, forms their initial impression of you and determines whether they would recommend you as an employer to their peers (potentially the cheapest form of recruitment).

In a public-sector organisation I work with, we do an annual 'Friends and Family'(F&F) test to see if our people would recommend our services to their own families. Employers could do the same thing with their employees. Be warned, as a low F&F test result probably means that you are going to start losing staff if you are not already. It's easier to improve your internal branding with the existing staff. According to an opinion piece in the marketing website 'The Drum', trust is the key to brand management, and 84% of people trust peer to peer recommendations over any other source of information. So, I will reiterate that retention starts with recruitment, and good recruitment leads to good retention.

We live in a world of first impressions. Brands live, and die, based on these impressions, not only in a B2C sense but more importantly how they are perceived by individuals who could potentially be interested in joining them. We have never been in such an age where impressions of an organisation or company can circulate so quickly around the talent pool. Websites such as vault.com and glassdoor.com even provide potential employees with real reviews from current employees and those who have gone through the interview process. Any employer who doesn't think of themselves as a brand in the talent market and doesn't apply similar principles to how they attract both employees and customers are going to be left behind.

Now I can see what you are thinking. Sure, if we are XYZ Inc., then we need to think about this, but what if we are Google or Microsoft or Amazon. 'I bet we don't have to do this, after all, we will attract 100,000 applications for every role in the company'. My answer is that you have just missed the point. They have *already* done this, which is why they have 100,000 people applying for every role. They are the most attractive employers to work for because they have created such a brand.

One of my favourite quotes, which by the way has been attributed to several key influencers, is 'There are three kinds of people in the world: those who make things happen, those who watch things happen, and those who wonder what happened'. I think it applies to companies as much as it does to individuals. You can place your company in the first category if you want to. It's not about having the hottest product, as what's hot today will be cold tomorrow; it's about having the most alluring proposition for talent. Remember that one person largely developed the original iPod design.

You don't need to be Google or Facebook; you just need to create a sustainable brand as a recognised, leading employer in your field. Let's face it. In 10 years, Google or Facebook might not even exist, but even if we go back 30 years, the same principles applied. Growing up, I was interested in hotel management as a career option, and I clearly remember my father saying to me 'Well if you want to go into hotel management, you need to get on the graduate scheme of "Trust House Forte (THF)"'. THF no longer exists, but it was then a shining employer brand – an industry leader and the default destination for a leisure industry graduate in the same way Marks and Spencer (M&S) was for retail. My point is that you don't need to be a cutting-edge technology player or the latest social craze to be an employer brand of choice. You need to be respected as an employer, treat people with respect and be consistent in the way you bring people into the organisation.

One of the most important factors when creating your employer brand is that it must be an honest reflection of your business, ethics and culture. It is pointless attracting someone to your organisation if the second they walk through the door, they are faced with an entirely different reality from the picture you portrayed.

I have a theory about M&S's – steady decline over the past two decades, from "The" High Street brand to "A N Other" . It's my theory, and I have no real evidence to back it up, and I am sure some retail analysts will be able to provide a totally different opinion using pie charts and graphs and probably an app these days. The theory is as follows: M&S used to provide a full range of services to its staff instore from doctors to hairdressers, which made it easy for employees to maintain their health and, more importantly, to return to work. There was a cohort of 'M&S Women' – experienced, returning to work mothers who were only available to join the workforce because of these other services being provided. These experienced women capable of relating to the core M&S customers and also mentor and train younger staff and trainee managers became the company's greatest assets. They were happy to be at work and serve the customers, and the customers were happy to be in the store because of how welcome they felt and the service they got.

Then came along a management consultant who advised M&S that it was much cheaper to let the employees have a sick day to go to the doctor than have a doctor instore. The benefits were withdrawn, and the potential labour pool was, therefore, reduced because M&S was no longer a viable option for busy mothers.

Now the times have changed, and thankfully, working women these days are able to work and deliver excellence in every conceivable role, not just aspire to be an M&S shop assistant, but the same principles still apply. If you look after your workforce, you will gain a reputation for looking after your workforce, and your potential talent pool, therefore, will increase in size.

Daniel Priestley, a business author, has written several well-regarded business programmes. *Oversubscribed*, one of the programmes, is aimed at making companies' sales of products more successful, but if you think about it, it deals with exactly what Facebook or Google are with their talent situation. They have what everyone wants – roles with the organisation that people want to be part of.

Regardless of whether a candidate is successful or not, the recruitment process and how they are treated will impact both their views of the firm and the views of others. It does not take long for feedback to reach the wider market. If the process is poor, the firm could be disregarded by other potential employees.

Kenneth Clarke, not the former Chancellor of the Exchequer but the writer and presenter of the wonderful TV programme *Civilisation,* concluded that the hallmark of a great civilisation is institutionalised courtesy. In this regard, an organisation that has regard for the feelings of others.

Companies that attract and retain staff are those that are progressive, responsive and dynamic, not only in the work that they do but also in the way they recruit. However, front-line operational staff rarely have time to dedicate to a fast and accurate recruitment process, as they are too busy serving customers to devote time for recruitment.

I once spoke to the manager of a mid-sized food supermarket, with about 15 tills and around 30 customer-facing staff on duty. I noticed that only 10 out of the 15 tills were operating, and the rest of the staff were refilling shelves on the shop floor or serving customers at specialist counters, and the lines at the tills were increasing in length. I asked him why he didn't take five staff off replenishing shelves and put them on the tills to reduce the backlog, and he replied, 'It's simple. Those in the queue have already got their products, and it's highly unlikely they will walk away from the trolley they have spent an hour filling just because they have to wait for 5 minutes to check out. Whereas those customers still on the shop floor can only put things in their trolleys in the first place if the products exist on the shelves'. He felt that the best way to serve his customers was to put more emphasis on the 'back office' and replenish the stocks than serve them quickly at the tills.

The same lesson can be applied to talent acquisition. If you constantly are too busy to recruit, then you will never grow because you already are too busy to recruit, and you can only grow through recruitment. It's a vicious circle.

A major misconception is that the shorter the interview process, the higher the chance of hiring the employee. I don't believe this. Over the past few years, we have been asking all our candidates what they are looking for when selecting their next employer. Congenial work and money are at the top of the list, but there are other factors.

- Feeling valued throughout the recruitment process irrespective of whether it leads to a successful appointment or not.
- Being provided accurate information on the company, practice and personalities at all stages of the interview process.
- Being provided specific interview arrangements – pre-planned time and place – and assistance in travel arrangements.
- Being provided fast and accurate feedback on all stages of the interview process.
- Being accorded the opportunity to meet peers in their specific department or practice area.

Only a very small percentage of the candidates were concerned about the time the recruitment process took, the majority of whom were currently unemployed or facing redundancy or uncertainty in their current position.

Whilst the points above may be perceived as 'nannying', the reality of the global talent market is that it is a seller's market for individuals with the requisite skills – after all, a company can only grow by expanding its talent pool. Good candidates have the luxury of picking their employer; therefore, the recruitment process must be extremely professional.

Companies can try to compete financially, but as Tom Clancy, a former Managing Partner of Accenture, once said, 'Money buys only time, not loyalty. A company that competes for talent strictly on cash is vulnerable to the next big offer. This game of escalating salaries is like an arms race – expensive and, ultimately, difficult, if not impossible to win'.

Chapter 2 – Types of Recruitment

Suppose an employee resigns, or a new position is created. There needs to be some recruitment activity to fill the vacancy. For the sake of argument, assume you are large enough to have someone to look after this (if you don't, then the same principles apply, but you might have to outsource or bring in a specialist interim or contractor). Let's look at the potential options.

Internal Recruitment Programmes

There is quite possibly someone already in the business waiting to step up, maybe a deputy or someone from another part of the business. As a rule, you should always try and promote from within unless you are seeking a brand-new skill set that doesn't exist in your business currently. It does, of course, mean you have to backfill. I have had clients tell me, 'I have the perfect person, and they want this role, but I can't afford to lose them from their current role'. Well, not moving them does not solve the problem; it just means you will probably end up with two roles to fill when your colleague decides that you don't value them, as you didn't give them the role, and leaves.

Why do I say promoting from within is better? First, the candidate knows the organisation, and, therefore, any transition period will be much less painful. They should be able to get a better handover from the existing incumbent if they already have a professional relationship. They will be motivated because you have listened to them and helped progress their career how they wanted it to. Finally, you get the best of both worlds because they still know their old role, which means it's much less risky to hire someone to replace them because they are still around, and if the hiring decision is wrong, you don't have a catastrophic loss of knowledge from your organisation.

So how should you do this internal recruitment? First, if you are in a large organisation, you should advertise the role internally. Just because you have your eye on someone does not mean that they are the only relevant candidate for that role. It also demonstrates to your organisation that you always do your due diligence with decisions that can affect the future of the company.

You should run the same interview process internally as externally (we will come to this later in the book) – the same assessments, interviews, exercises. This is important because of the following:

        a) It reaffirms your decision; and

        b) It reaffirms to both the employee and their peers that they achieved the role on their merit and capabilities and no other reason. This is especially important in appointing 'Deputies' who step up to the main job.

Obviously, if you are a small company (less than c.20 people), it will probably be clear who the heir apparent should be, but I would still interview the person for the role if nothing to bottom out any concerns they have about stepping up.

Ideas for Internal Recruitment Programmes

You will know already know the candidates in internal recruitment programmes, so it's not always easy to accurately assess them in the same dispassionate way as external candidates. Assuming you only have internal candidates, the following are some suggestions of exercises you could set as a part of the assessment process:

- To design a new company logo reflecting your product and brand values;
- To write a new company strapline/slogan;
- To prepare a one-page executive summary of a briefing document; and
- To design a new product or service for the company.

External Peer-Peer/Employee Referral Programmes

I have deliberately split external recruitment into a few categories. Earlier we learnt that 84% of people rely on peer to peer information than any other source. In other words, if you have 10 people in your company, you potentially have 10 marketers who can help your source talent. Peer to peer referrals is the gold standard of recruitment programmes.

If you have a strong employee referral programme, then the majority of your recruitments should be done for you. If you are being recommended by your employees to their peers and connections, then you know you have a good employer brand. If this is the situation for your organisation, then put this book down, go, celebrate and come back to this book when the situation changes.

There are a variety of ways to motivate your team to refer vacancies to their networks, and some examples are as follows:

- **Money** – A financial reward, maybe a percentage of what you would pay an external provider, is a strong incentive; however, it should not be the primary motivator. If you have to rely on hard currency, then you probably haven't built a strong enough employer brand yet, so you might want to revisit that first.
- **Social rewards** – Hard-to-find concert tickets, an amazing meal at a top restaurant or maybe something substantial such as an engraved watch are relevant options. If you gave someone a £5,000 watch rather than £5,000 in cash, every time they look at the watch, probably for years ahead, they will think of your company in a positive light.
- **Team incentives** – If you have departments in your organisation, you could have a competition about how many employee referrals they can achieve in a quarter with some sort of team away day for the highest performing team.
- **Charitable donations** – A charitable donation to a cause selected by the referrer is another option. With this, you also have the added benefit to include this in your Corporate Social Responsibility Programme.

What I will say is that if you haven't followed similar principles to those outlined in Sandy Asch's book, then you are unlikely to have a strong enough brand to be able to rely on this channel.

External Recruitment – Outside Sources

External recruitment seems simple but, in fact, is highly complex and where most firms waste money and make mistakes.

There are two ways to do it – you can either do it yourself or with a third-party provider. Then within the latter, there are various methodologies you can use – Executive Search, Contingent Agency Recruitment, Advertised Selection. We need to break this down a bit and highlight the benefits and challenges or risks of both.

There is a growing trend for firms to try and 'in-source' their recruitment and rely less on external agencies. Frankly, I applaud this. Why you ask. Well, in my view, many external providers charge far too much to recycle a CV from LinkedIn, and those firms leave the client wondering exactly where the added value is. It is, therefore, completely right that the client should seek to build their own function to source great talent from this cost-effective source. In fact, JCM trains client teams to do exactly this. There are, however, limits to this activity, and the clients who think that having built this team now give an 'in-house executive search capability' are often sadly mistaken.

Using a Provider

First, you have to select your recruitment partner(s), but all recruitment firms can look the same to an inexpert eye. They are not. Forget about the glossy websites, the talks of hundreds of professionals they have in their global practices, the amazing database of talent they have and ask the following two questions:

- Tell me about the last five similar positions you have recruited for; and
- Introduce me to the exact team who will be working on this project.

Don't worry about terms and conditions and fee rates at this stage, as they are all negotiable and will all fall into the same sort of brackets eventually. You need to be confident that you are not being sold 'the Partner' and then being served by 'the Associate' and they understand your business and, more importantly, your business culture.

Once you have selected your external firm, then go through the terms and conditions because there can be significant differences.

Expenses: Some firms will try and charge you expenses on top of their professional fees. I am not talking about large expenses, such as those of airline tickets to go and interview candidates, but a fixed % of the fee to cover 'administration'. This is an archaic practice, generally enforced by the larger traditional firms, and it's nonsense. It's purely a mechanism to increase profit margins, and I have seen some firms charge up to 8% of the total fee.

JCM doesn't charge its clients any expenses except exceptional expenses, such as travel, and any such sums are agreed in advance, itemised and recharged a cost

Stage payments: There is no problem with paying the fee in stages, and most quality firms will insist on an initial fee or retainer. We generally charge 1/3rd of our fees on the commencement of the project because it can take months until the next stage, and like any business, we have to ensure cash flow. However, once the first instalment is paid, the subsequent payments should be based on the deliverables. You should have a report or a shortlist or whatever stage you agree. Too many firms still try to charge stage payments on a time basis. I came across a client a few years ago who had paid out nearly £200k in stage payments and was yet to interview a single candidate.

Guarantees: Any search firm or agency confident in its ability will have absolutely no problem in guaranteeing an appointment for three months, and the better firms will guarantee for six months. This gives you the certainty that if the appointment doesn't work out because the candidate is not the right person for the role, then the firm will re-run the recruitment exercise at no additional costs to you.

The selection of the external needs is to be done by you and your colleagues, not led by a procurement department. I have responded to dozens of procurement requests in my career, and they all use the same stock questions around our policies, diversity targets, among others. Not one of them has ever effectively asked me to demonstrate our capability to understand our client's business or actually deliver the mandates that are going to be required.

JCM runs assessment panels for clients selecting recruitment partners, and we use interview-based techniques as if we are hiring a candidate. Once we have made our shortlist, we check functional items, such as the presence of indemnity insurance, diversity policies, to name a few.

If you do this properly, you can build a partnership with your external provider. Note that I am not using the word 'supplier' here. You don't want a supplier. A supplier is for stationary or furniture or printer toner cartridges. Suppliers sell you commodities and send you a box of Quality Street at Christmas. When you are talking about talent, you don't want to be sold to, and you don't want a commodity.

A true partnership model will build a relationship between you and your external consultant to the point that they emotionally invest in your business and your journey. This is where the magic happens, and this is where you start saving. If you trust your recruitment partner, you don't need to spend time reading stacks of CVs; you can just accept that the candidates presented are competent and have them booked into your diary. If you trust your recruitment partner's knowledge of your business, you don't need to spend much time briefing every time a role comes up. If you don't think that your recruitment partner is trying to sell to you, you can use their wise counsel when making the tough decision between two excellent candidates.

In the best recruitment processes I have been a part of and witnessed, the recruitment partner's job does not end when the shortlist is done. They have sat in the room or even taken an active part in the interview process, then guided the discussions amongst the key stakeholders after the interviews. My clients and I have often joked that they need to print me a security pass and find me a desk as I am in the building so often during a recruitment campaign.

I could write a whole book on supplier selection (maybe the difficult second book), but let me sum it up for you here in some key points:
- Know what you are committing to and what they are committing to;
- Make sure you both have a clear understanding who is doing what in the process;
- Make sure the rewards are tied to deliverables; and
- Remember, this consultant is going to represent your brand in the marketplace. Do they exude your brand values?

Methods

As we have already discussed, there are several methods of recruitment, utilising different mediums, some of which are more suited to a particular set of requirements than others.

Head Hunting or Executive Search (to give it its more respectable title)

Head-hunting is probably the most accurate way to identify suitable candidates for an organisation. This does not, however, mean it is a suitable solution for all situations. Headhunting is time-consuming but can produce optimum results against a specific brief. It is certainly not always the most cost-effective solution for hiring junior to middle management personnel, and we would generally recommend it only for individual senior appointments that cannot be sourced elsewhere and for highly sensitive positions.

Many clients ask me why they can't do this themselves. Simply put, whether this activity is done internally or externally, remember that sourcing/identifying candidates is only 30% of the process. Some firms and most internal teams rely purely on web resources such as LinkedIn, which is indeed a powerful tool for identifying and approaching candidates. Last time I checked, however, it was inadequate at keeping candidates motivated throughout a six-month recruitment process, and it's terrible at negotiations. You cannot replace an experienced talent consultant with a database however strong its CRM functions are.

Executive search is not about finding the talent. Anyone with an internet connection can do it these days. It's about a comprehensive candidate assessment and benchmarking exercise. It's a candidate care exercise, keeping the shortlist motivated during a 3-, 6-, 12-month selection process. It's about providing insight and knowledge on the market for the duration of the search, not pushing the first candidate past the finishing post. It's about advising the client when they are wrong and suggesting constructive ways forward.

The reason clients should be paying the extra % for an executive search is simple – they are paying for years of experience, years of lessons learnt. Too many times I see clients repurpose HR professionals into recruiters and expect them to provide a similar service as an experienced search professional. That's like asking a bus driver to take a spin in Lewis Hamilton's Mercedes and win the Monaco Grand Prix.

If companies truly want an executive search function, then build an executive search function. That involves hiring experienced search professionals to lead it, not re-tasking HR or internal recruitment managers. A few firms have done this over the years, and it has paid massive dividends. PA Consulting set up a Partner Recruitment Acquisition team back in the 1990s, staffed by experienced executive search personnel and led by Roselyn Cason-Marcus, my good friend, who now leads Partner Acquisition for McKinsey &Co. Over the years, they saved literally millions of pounds on executive search fees because they used external providers for less than 10 % of their open partner positions.

Other firms have tried on a more basic budget, and whilst I wouldn't say they have failed, they certainly haven't fulfilled their potential.

For years people have asked me if I am worried about the impact of the internet with sites such as LinkedIn on my business. My answer is no because they are not taking the market share of my business. They have taken market share from the low-end contingent market, and rightly so, as why should a client pay 20-25% for a CV from an active job seeker that's readily available online? We would encourage, support and train our clients' teams to reduce their spending on that channel.

Clients also ask me whether technology will replace the need for executive search. More and more articles are appearing about the great work that IBM's Watson, among others, is doing in the field of recruitment and how soon executive search will be obsolete. Sorry Skynet, but we have had this prediction before, with the internet in general, then Monster, then LinkedIn. If anything, technology seems to provide a growth spurt to the numbers of recruiters, not a reduction.

Now don't get me wrong – I am a technologist, and I believe technology plays an essential role in the talent management lifecycle. Technology helps the human element avoid mistakes; it securely collates and distributes data; it schedules accurately and provides analytical data at the end of the campaign. It enhances rather than degrade the humanist aspects of the process.

Technology cannot totally replace the human input because we are dealing with humans. These days finding candidates and analysing their CVs into a long list probably only accounts for 10% of the role. The human process management, the cultural fit assessment (more important than ever before to both candidates and companies these days) and the hand holding through the process are roles a machine cannot take on in the foreseeable future. I bet even Google doesn't have an algorithm to measure 'Googliness' (1/4 of their selection criteria).

Would you want to work for a company that selects you purely by a computer algorithm?

The issue with any system is that it is generally designed by engineers. The issue with most recruitment systems seems to be that they are designed by engineers and HR personnel, and unfortunately, HR is a different discipline from recruitment.

Don't get me wrong. I applaud the amazing work these engineers and machines are doing, but don't write off humanity yet.

Advertised Selection Campaigns

Companies' greatest problem in times of growth is often the lack of quality candidates who are physically coming through the door. Many smaller firms have the added problem that they do not currently command a high profile amongst candidates in the marketplace. Therefore, a solution to this for growing companies is to use some sort of advertising to boost their candidate throughput. Whilst advertisements can draw huge numbers of inappropriate candidates, generally good ones can result in one or two placements. The number of responses only becomes a factor when you do not have the back-office machinery in place to handle the process. By allowing for an element of advertising, you achieve three things. First, raising the company's profile amongst candidates and potential clients. Second, a greater throughput of candidates. Third, potential cost saving on agency and outside supplier's fees, if you run the process in-house. Selection is a very powerful tool when used well.

Historically, senior appointments were featured in broadsheet newspapers' appointment sections or on specific websites. Junior or technical roles were featured in specialist trade press or on high volume technology sites (and still are). I used to work for a company that made almost as much money out of selling job advertisements to the Sunday Times as they did actually placing people. These days clients have many more tools at their disposal.

Specialist online recruitment sites still heavily feature executive appointments; however, I would hypothesise that actually more senior recruitment is conducted on broader content sites, such as LinkedIn, than any other medium currently.

LinkedIn has a range of tools, many of which are aimed at the corporate in-house recruiter, and frankly, if your company and your role are attractive, all you should need is a good in-house recruiter to sift through the CVs and make the interview arrangements. If the cost of a LinkedIn advertisement is £500, then why wouldn't you try this channel first and save yourself £40k–100k of recruitment fees?

Many leading search firms will tell you that 'No one really good or senior will apply for a job on LinkedIn', and that may be true, but Bob might see the advertisement for a Senior VP of finance and just pick up the phone to call his former colleague Pam, who happens to be your current CFO and is running the advertisement. Just because someone doesn't reply to a specific email address doesn't mean that they haven't arrived via that channel.

My first question to a new executive search client is 'What have you done so far to source someone for this role'? If it's not a particularly sensitive role, and they haven't explored options such as LinkedIn, I will suggest that they do before they engage me. Why? Because there is nothing worse than being three days into a project, with a third of our fees paid, and then someone hearing about the role and contacting their old pal directly. Whilst technically we are fully entitled to our fee and probably a cancellation fee as well, it doesn't leave a nice taste in the mouth.

I have never charged a cancellation fee from a client in such a situation, and often, if we really haven't spent much time on a project, we will also give them some credit towards their next assignment on the basis that we are partners in their enterprise and the long-term client relationship is more important to us than any short-term gain.

This is not to be confused with clients who brief us, then continue to brief other firms and run their own campaign. We demand exclusivity on a project, not for financial reasons, but for the simple fact that if one person doesn't have control of the project, its likely to tip itself up and crash and burn.

Contingency Agency Recruitment

People in "blue-blooded" search firms tend to look down on contingency agencies with a mixture of pity and condescension. I have operated at the highest levels of the blue-blooded search arena and the highly commoditised contingency arena and have been successful in both. There is no qualitative difference between really good search firms and really good contingent firms. They are both capable of excellent work, but their function and methodologies are very different.

It's like comparing a shrimp fisherman, who uses a net, with a lobster fisherman, who uses a pot. Neither is better or worse; it just depends on what you want to catch as to how you go about it.

No recruitment company can claim to have total coverage of the marketplace in terms of the available active candidates, and so in order to secure your market share of CVs, you sometimes need to cast a 'wide net over as many agencies as practicable. Limiting yourself by too small of a preferred supplier list can cut a huge number of smaller independent firms out of the supply chain. As a result, you can potentially miss out on a large number of candidates.

Many companies find themselves overwhelmed by the number of random CVs they receive from agencies, and many of these are little more than rebadged LinkedIn profiles sent out on mailshots. I have received three CVs for technical developers this week from an agency, all of them for technical developers. I have never employed and can't ever see myself employing a technical developer. This can be avoided by a slick and effective process, in which outside suppliers only supply to requests. If you get the process right, then the number of agencies receiving those requests and sending you content becomes less relevant.

Contingency recruitment is a powerful tool that has both benefits and risks. Generally, higher volume campaigns for a large number of similarly skilled individuals lend themselves to contingency recruitment, but equally low volume campaigns seeking senior talent on a reactive basis can lend themselves to contingency methods. If you don't have a burning platform or a specific date when you must appoint someone, then maybe a passive contingency campaign to see what's available on the market is suitable.

Pros
- Casts a wide net over the talent pool; and
- No direct costs (we will revisit this later in the book) involved unless you hire someone.

Cons
- You don't get exclusivity on the candidates; and
- It's hard to build a partnership with your supplier.

Graduate/MBA Milk round

Many companies make the mistake of treating the recruitment of graduates from top universities as similar to normal recruitment. Graduates from top universities and business schools have a wealth of information and opportunities supplied to them. They can pick and choose their next company. In order to address this area, companies must have a unique offering that attracts graduates and MBAs. The first approach must be to target the university staff, add value to their offerings by making personnel available for talks and lectures, sponsor events and provide resources. The second approach must be directed at the students, by providing literature and digital content initially, followed up by visits by both senior and junior personnel with similar backgrounds on special recruitment days. Also, providing graduate placement schemes for vacation periods, sponsorship of studies, fun-days and, also, opportunities for MBA students to work on projects alongside existing teams can be beneficial.

Specialist Programmes

It is not uncommon these days for companies to have the need for a specialist recruitment programme. This could be because they need people with very specific new technology skills or, more commonly, have an issue with something like diversity. In fact, this is so common now that Sandra Guzman and Nathalie Mawdsley, my good friends and colleagues, left the mainstream executive search world to establish a specialist diversity consultancy – Unida Consulting. They assist clients with this very issue from both thought leadership and practical perspective. I would strongly recommend anyone interested in this topic to check out some of their excellent content at http://www.unidaconsulting.com/

If your company finds itself in such a situation, then my strongest recommendation is to bring in the experts, whoever they may be. Trying to fix the situation yourself is likely to fail, considering that the shortfall developed under your watch in the first place. Remember that everything we are trying to do here is to build your employer brand. If you launch a new product, you will advertise it – you need to be thinking along the same lines here.

Foreign Hire Programmes

People sometimes forget that there are some amazing talent pools elsewhere of both foreign talent but also potential returnee talent. The economic conditions in one geographic area might have prompted talent to shift abroad, but maybe it's time for that talent to come back. Your challenge, which really is stating the obvious, is logistics. You need to think about this in the following three areas:

- How are you going to interview?

- How are you going to relocate the successful candidates?
- How are you going to treat people who may have to return if visa rules change?

I would strongly advise involving a specialist partner who can utilise the resources of the local market that you are trying to target. Every situation will be different, and you may have to grapple with the complexity of mapping international qualifications and professional registrations.

Think this strategy through very carefully. In my experience, this can provide a relatively quick short-term fix; however, this migratory talent pool is likely to move onto the next favourable geographical area as the economic cycle progresses.

Chapter 3 – The True Costs of Recruitment

Ask someone how much it costs to recruit an employee, and they would probably say that 'It cost us x £s for the advertisement', or 'We had to pay an agency 23%'. The actual answer is slightly more complex because people generally forget about their and their own staff time involved in the process.

A more accurate cost, therefore, is as follows:

(a)   The cost of the recruitment medium + (b) The cost of the employers own staff time

Now how many of you actually know what you cost? I am not talking about the cost of employing you, your wages, insurance but the cost of you doing a task for a business. For a salesperson, this is relatively easy to work out. There are approximately 260 working days in a calendar year, take out 10% for holidays, sickness, training, among others, and you are left with approximately 234 working days. If a salesman's target is £1m a year, then their daily cost is as follows:

£1,000,000 / 234 = £4,473

Therefore. The hourly cost of this individual conducting interviews rather than selling your product is £534

For individuals who don't hold such a target, it should still be possible to work out what their value is to the business is each year (if you can't, then you probably don't need them) and subsequently, a daily and hourly rate.

This exercise is very valuable, and I would encourage companies to do it for all their employees. It's one of the most powerful metrics available to you in business, as you can instantly understand the cost of an away day, holding a weekly meeting, running a special internal project, but we are digressing; let's get back to talent!

Now having established the base cost, we need to count in additional factors such as the following:
-    The cost of having an interim whilst the role is vacant;
-    The cost on the productivity of having the role vacant; and
-    The additional load that affects the other employees of having the role vacant.

All the above need to be multiplied by the number of days until the new employee joins.

I would hazard an educated guess that on an average the true cost of recruiting someone, especially a replacement of someone, is at least **140-150%** of their first year's actual cost.

It's rather important then that this be sorted. You do it efficiently; you do it professionally, and make your process stand out amongst your competitors.

Duplication

Another hidden cost of recruitment is duplication. It really occurs only in larger firms who are looking for similar profiles across multiple geographies. But when it does happen, it is rife! I once came across an instance of one of the world's top 4 professional services firms who was running the same search out of 8 different geographic locations.

Concerning a middle management role these days, you have to consider your talent pool to be at least regional if not global. The organisation mentioned above had a regional structure in place, but local hiring even at the £500k + level was done locally. Five different executive search firms (yes, some firms were retained more than once) had been mandated with retainers of c.£25,000 and were all searching for the same profile of the individual. When we looked deeper into the process, we found there was over a 30% overlap of shortlisted candidates across the five shortlists. Irrespective of who got hired, the firm was going to be paying five firms for either completing or cancelling the searches.

The fact that there was no co-ordination meant that the firm was going to waste nearly £400,000 just on a single recruitment. When we analysed their overall £50m annual spending, we identified savings of nearly £10m within a few hours of looking at the data by eliminating duplication.

Chapter 4 – The Recruitment Process

So, what does good look like? Fast is not necessarily good; neither is cheap nor expensive. Good is efficient; good treats people with respect and the way you would want to be treated. Whether you are hiring a CEO or a security guard, the basic principles remain the same.

Every business has a process. Julian Thomas and Andrew Williams of Maisha & Co, my good friends and both ex-senior partners of Big 4 consulting firms, can talk to you about the process for weeks on end. I am no expert, but what I have learnt in the past twenty odd years is that if there is a good process, then the outcome is immeasurably more likely to be positive than if you make it up as you go.

At the end of this chapter, you will see some diagrams (who doesn't love diagrams) outlining the suggested stages in the process for junior, mid-senior and senior candidates. You'll notice that they basically come down to five distinct stages. I will gladly challenge anyone who says that you need more than this. I have placed very senior £1m+ individuals in five stages or less, and I have also experienced the 27-stage process for the same level of individual. The only difference – one started 12 months sooner and had already made his organisation £10m by the time other candidate had agreed on a start date.

I think its fear that makes people add stages – fear that they will be the one making the decision, fear that if it's the wrong decision, then they are going to suffer. If that's truly the culture of your organisation, then you have bigger problems than recruitment.

My plea to hiring managers, therefore, is to please be bold. You will make mistakes. It happens, get over it, because the paralysis of not hiring someone and waiting for all your colleagues to agree is killing the growth of your company.

Do you think Mark Zuckerberg, Larry Ellison or Richard Branson put their potential executive hires through 27 rounds of interviews? Of course, they don't.

The other important part of the process, before we get down to the detail, is your employer brand. See, that's cropped up again strangely enough. Now I know that you are a very important and busy person, with lots of client commitments and very important meetings to attend. That does not give you the right to stand a candidate up or cancel a meeting with them half an hour before its due to start. That's not you being an important busy person; that's you being a schmuck (I would have used a strong word here, but my publisher wouldn't let me). You have no idea what your candidate has had to do to make their diary work for this meeting. They too might have important client commitments or important meetings. They also have the added disadvantage of having to 'disappear' from their current employment to talk to you, a competitor. What are they supposed to say when their Boss finds them at their desk and says, 'Emily I thought you were at the dentist this afternoon?' 'Oh yes, Sarah, he cancelled because he was busy?'

I have had clients who have stood people up, without reason, three times. No pre-warning, they just either don't dial into the call or don't show up for the meeting. It's rude; it's inconsiderate, and more importantly, it tarnishes your 'Employer Brand'. So, at the end of the week, when Emily is at Corny & Barrow with her two friends, recounting the week's events and being asked about her interview at ZZZ consulting, and she tells her two eminently qualified friends that she was stood up for the meeting, you have probably just lost two more people from your potential talent pool. But you haven't just lost two people because they might tell their friends about how arrogant the management at ZZZ is, and one of those people will probably blog about it on glassdoor.com or vault.com.

When you drop even the tiniest stone into a still pond of water, it never enters without a ripple.

Whenever I do executive search these days, I follow a rule. Two strikes, and you're out. What I mean by this is if the candidate is stood up two times throughout the interview process, then I will recommend to the candidate to withdraw from the process because this client clearly does not respect them. More importantly I will tell the client I am doing it as well!

Now, life happens; things in diaries move; mistakes are made, but they don't have to be an issue. My 'respect' test happens when the client rings me and says, 'I can't make it, or I was stuck in a meeting, but I would like to ring the candidate myself and explain that and make a new arrangement.' When that happens, I know its genuine. I respect the client, but more importantly, the candidate respects the client.

We are going to move on now to some more specific bits of advice around the process. If you are a CEO or not the individual who actually runs the recruitment process, then feel free to skip this bit and come back later when your recruiter comes back with a plan, so you can see what good looks like.

Planning

Most recruitment practices follow the same basic principle and happen in the following four main stages:

- Identification of need and production of material;
- Decision of recruitment methods;
- Actual recruitment process; and
- Feedback evaluation and review.

Identification of Need and Production of Material

If you are replacing an employee, identification of need is simple – we have lost an HR director; therefore, we need an HR director. However, it's always good practice when a vacancy occurs to ask the question 'Do we still need an X in that role'? Sometimes companies evolve and grow tremendously since the initial role was created, and the absence of someone gives an ideal opportunity to review the current shape of the organisation.

When I am working with clients, the easiest way I follow to establish the level of need is to find out how easy it is for someone to write a job description for the role that is not a generic 'HR Director' job description copied from the internet, but a tailored document concerning the individual organisation and challenges to be faced.

Production of Job Descriptions and Person Specification

Whilst each hire is individual, many similar skilled candidates may be hired in a year in some situations. In order to minimise repeated work and speed up the process, draft job descriptions and person specifications should be prewritten. This will mean that only a small amount of time to update the basic specification will be required in order to fit it into a particular role.

Even if this is not the case, every key person in the organisation should be asked to write their job description. It's a useful exercise and can be used to build career development plans for your staff. We often find with clients who have grown quickly that formal job descriptions have never existed, so I would strongly encourage this situation be rectified sooner rather than later, and who better to write a job description than the person currently doing the job!

The core of job descriptions and person specifications should be standard for your organisation and contain similar base information so that they are familiar to the staff and managers who provide the core material for their detail.

They should contain as much information as possible; however, as a minimum, the following must be included:

Job Description	**Person Specification**
Job Title	Personal Attributes
Company Description / Overview of the Opportunity	Qualifications or Experience
	Special Clearances (Security)
Line responsibilities	Specialist Knowledge
External responsibilities	Mobility
Salary and Remuneration	
Location	

Let me give you an example of a combined job description and person specification. The company is a management consultancy firm called Flipper, and the role is for a Technical Architect. You will notice in the example below that some information is repeated. The overall description is the scene setter and may well contain nearly all the information contained in the formal specification document.

Job Description and Person Specification – Technical Architect

A technical architect at Flipper is one step away from Partner, Partner being the most senior role within the business. We are looking for a number of candidates to fill positions at this level who have established business contacts within the London area.

By comparison to other firms, Flipper positions itself between strategy firms such as McKinsey and Bain and implementation firms such as Accenture and IBM. We work with Fortune 500 clients taking projects from insight to implementation; therefore it is imperative that candidates have real hands-on consulting experience and are be able to provide evidence of delivering consultancy work through teams of consulting or operational staff. Candidates must be able to demonstrate a combination of IT and business experience and will typically be selling and managing assignments to bring in revenue of around £1.5million per year.

Our Information Technology group began to develop business in the UK around 6 months ago having spent a large chunk of time during 1998 scoping opportunities. We have so far sold assignments in London, Glasgow, Liverpool and Wales.

In preparation for this relative 'start-up', we have relocated 16 consulting staff from France, including a Senior Partner who has accepted the challenge of Head of the UK IT Practice. Many of these 12 have chosen to locate from our Bracknell office, and we need strong business development capability to begin to feed the assignment work.

Flipper is a global firm, and for any major UK assignments to date, we have seconded resource from the US and other parts of the world as well as proactively recruited UK based resources. To date we have added 4 new joiners to our team this year.

This opportunity will appeal to consultants who are looking to make Partner in a consulting firm and excited by being relied upon to be entrepreneurial and challenged by the prospect of developing business in a 'start-up' environment. Building on an established contact base and market insights must be good enough to bring things to the table.

The Flipper organisation is not hierarchical; we all pull together to get work done, and even our Partners have utilisation targets. We believe in staff development at every level and are committed to fostering ongoing professional growth. At the Technical Architect level, we expect that people will want to succeed and be promoted to Partner.

We have a unique compensation scheme; Flipper is owned by its employees, and our compensation policies are designed to give everyone a significant equity stake in the companies' continued success.

INFORMATION TECHNOLOGY – STRATEGY

Technical Architect

Position Rank: Director

Role Profile

Tasks: Key account management, team leadership, bid and assignment management, selling, development of senior-level contacts within client organisations. Maybe a technical authority. Training: Business Management, Key Account Management and Management of large, complex assignments.

Development:

> *Role 1 – Operator/Assignment Manager/Project Manager/Director. Maybe called upon to operate in a locum line/functional role.*
>
> *Role 2 – Specialist, selective operating, bringing technical expertise to the assignment at all levels beyond that of the other team members. Increasingly called upon to speak or write in specialist areas.*
>
> *Role 3 – Defined sales/account management and development responsibilities. May have a client/sector/geographic focus for sales activity.*

Education/Qualifications: Good technical degree or business degree or equivalent with an IT specialisation, from a leading educational institution or blue-chip training programme.

Technical Expertise: 5–10 years of experience in some of the following technology environments:

- *IT strategy and delivery;*
- *Planning and the subsequent management in the engineering of IT into the design of new business processes;*
- *Application and promotion of Information Management techniques;*
- *Design of technical architectures and applications portfolios in a client/server, distributed processing environment (including GroupWare, Internet etc.); and*
- *Application and promotion of benefits management techniques.*

Sector Experience: Experience in Finance and Transportation is particularly useful.

Personal Profile:

The candidate should demonstrate the following qualities:

- *Goal orientated;*
- *Effective self-starter;*

- *Good communicator, both oral and written;*
- *Excellent relationship builder;*
- *Self-confident and motivational of others;*
- *Ambition (but co-operative);*
- *Stamina and drive; and*
- *Ability to rapidly absorb new knowledge and combine both theory and practice.*

The candidate should also possess the following:
- *First class consulting skills; and*
- *Proven sales and business development skills.*

The candidate must also be willing to travel extensively and be prepared to work long hours often. Residence within easy distance of one of our office locations is also preferable.

Location: London, England

Compensation
- *Salaries are industry competitive, based on qualifications and experience.*
- *Bonus opportunity based on individual performance and company profitability.*
- *Benefits package including medical, dental, 401(k) retirement plan, life, and long-term disability insurance.*

The above description is comprehensive. It sells the company, as well as the role, and provides all the relevant information for someone to assess whether they meet the criteria. However, you will also notice that a lot of it is reusable for any role in the organisation. There is no point trying to reinvent the wheel every time you go and recruit a new person.

Production of Supporting Recruitment Material

To ensure that candidates feel comfortable and informed throughout the process, a presentation pack, which is given to the candidate when invited to the first interview, should be made available. Now it could be in the digital form on a recruitment microsite, a brochure or a presentation. I am going to use the word 'pack', but you can apply this to any medium you have chosen for your recruitment campaign.

The pack should vary in content depending on the area of business and level of the role. The packs should be pre-prepared and, where possible, personalised for the particular job specification. The best way to achieve this is with a folder type brochure that contains standard company information, with a loose leave file section into which specific information can be inserted. If in the digital form, an overall slide deck can be created, and then the irrelevant slides can be deleted. The following is a guideline that I would suggest as the minimum requirements:

- Company brochure;
- Flowchart of the recruitment process;
- Organisation chart of the company;
- Relevant company press releases and general marketing;
- Compensation and benefits arrangements;
- Outline of the specific department;
- Summaries of product details if relevant;
- Full job description and person specification; and
- Contact details.

Now for a more senior role, you might want to include the following as well:

- Summary of company accounts;
- Named organisation chart of the company; and
- Shareholding structure and arrangements.

The most important thing to remember is to maintain consistency in the information provided. There is nothing worse than a candidate being provided with a pack of information, which is wildly different from that displayed on the company's website or in the public domain.

I would like to add a note on 'apps'. I have seen companies trying and developing apps for the recruitment of their candidates, which give them status updates on their progress, links to company information, among others. These apps don't cost much to develop these days but be warned, as you have to be very confident in the quality and quantity of information going into the background of the app to make it functional and updated if you don't want it to become a demonstration of how inefficient your organisation is.

Personally, I would suggest you leave the apps to Starbucks to order your coffee.

The Decision on Recruitment Methodology

The decision on recruitment methodology will set the tone of your entire recruitment process. It is important to remember that you are not carving this decision in a stone tablet and displaying it in the reception of your company. If the first decision does not work out, then be brave, change it and start again. Now I am not going to fall into the trap that writers do and give you the definition of insanity (I may have just fallen into the trap), but time and time again, I see clients doggedly sticking to a methodology because it has worked before. The world moves on, and every recruitment scenario should be approached with fresh eyes and on its individual merits.

Unfortunately, I cannot sit here and give you a set of cast iron scenario rules as to when you should or should not use a certain method. We have previously discussed the main methods at your disposal. The following are some guidelines as to how not make the decision:

- Do not make the decision based on cost;
- Do not utilise the same method just because it has worked before; and
- Do not ignore the advice of your trusted advisor (By all means, disagree but at least listen).

The Recruitment and Assessment Process

'Finally, we get to the main event', I hear you say. Trust me; if you haven't taken heed of the steps above, then there is little point in implementing a process. Now I am going to let you in on a little secret. If you are manufacturing widgets, there is a fixed set of stages you have to go through from procuring the raw materials and producing the product to sending the finished commodity to your customers. It's a process, and it can be mapped quite easily, and the efficiencies can be identified. I will refer you now back to Chapter 2, as we are not dealing with a commodity. People are unpredictable and unique, and therefore, there is no such thing as a perfect recruitment process. What we can do, however, is provide you with an example template, which, if followed, will ensure you have at the very least a robust recruitment process that should ensure that the correct candidate is hired. For simplicity, I have 'assumed' external involvement in the form of an agency or search firm.

Now you may already have something like this in place, but do you actually use it? Does everyone in the process use it? Do hiring managers stick to it, or do they start inserting additional steps in the process when they like? More importantly, do your potential candidates know what it looks like?

In my experience, candidates will happily jump through any hoops you might like to place in front of them, as long as they know about it in advance.

At the start of the recruitment exercise, the process steps should have dates appended to them, and diaries and meeting rooms should be booked out at the start of the process on the assumption that everything will go according to the plan. After all, it's much easier to remove something from the diary than to put it in, and I don't know anyone who doesn't enjoy the occasional extra free hour that suddenly frees up in their diary when something gets cancelled.

The following are some example processes for different levels. Now, I am not claiming they are utopian processes that are going to work for every organisation. They are ideas to be adapted and developed to fit your company. All I will say is to keep it simple, as there is no need to over complicate the recruitment process if you are confident in your process.
- Design each stage to have a specific part of the process and outcome;
- Don't do rounds of repetitive interviews;

-    Build a schedule and diarise it at the start of the process;
-    Explain your processes to your candidates at the very first meeting; and
-    Treat your candidates' diary with as much respect as your own.

Junior / Graduate / MBA Recruitment – A Process

Junior / Graduate / MBA Recruitment – The Process

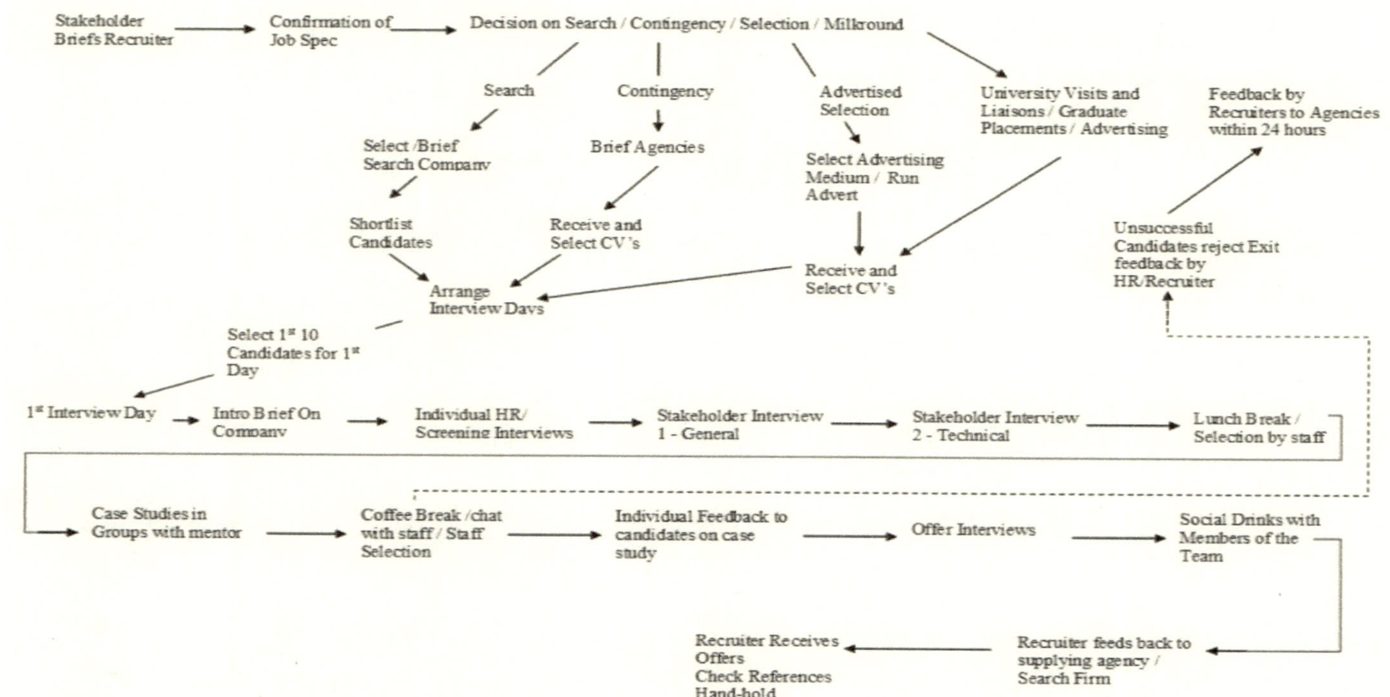

Middle Management Recruitment—The 5 Stage Process

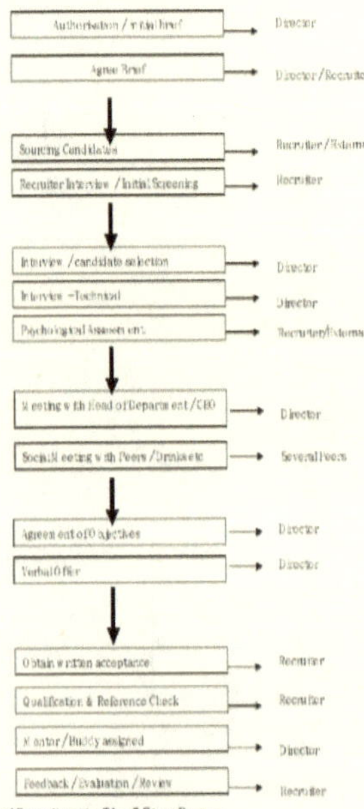

Director Level Recruitment—The 5 Stage Process

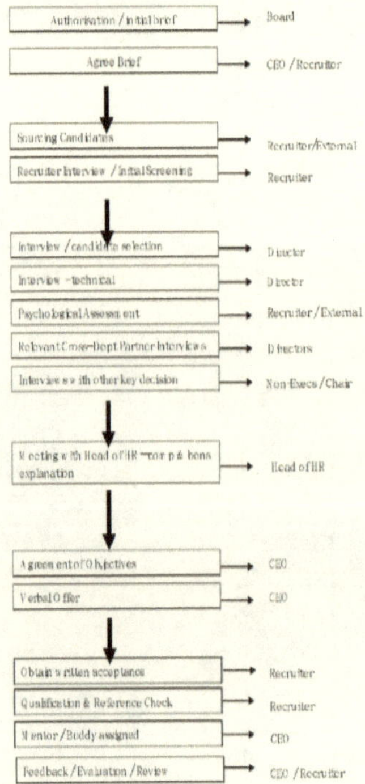

The Interview and Assessment Process

I have provided a nice flow chart above of what good can look like in the interview process, and even if I do say so myself, I think it's pretty clear, so I am not going to write pages on what the picture says. After all, a picture paints a thousand words.

However, I am going to labour on interviews from this point on. I am not going to list thousands of interview questions and case studies because that would just be cheating to get my word count up for my publisher. Instead, I am going to give you some rules to follow. I say rules, but I mean a rule – one rule; that's all you have to remember.

The rule is to 'make it count'. I know of a client who proudly states that no one joins his organisation unless they have completed 25 interviews. Wow, really? That's all I can say to that.

Let's just jump back a couple of chapters to 'The True Costs of Recruitment'. Do you remember the formula? In the above example, the daily rate of the individuals (all partners at a large accountancy firm) was a minimum of £4,000 per day. Each interview would last an hour and take 30 minutes for before and after preparation, feedback, travel, disruption in the diary, among others.

Therefore, on a conservative estimate, it has so far cost £25,000 just to interview a single candidate, excluding the cost of a scheduling team, PA's time, room costs or any external head-hunter fees. Assume that they have shortlisted four candidates, and that's a cool £100,000 spent without a single hire being made yet. Ouch!

Now, if these were specific interviews challenging various aspects of the candidate's technical competency and ability, then that would be a different matter. We put a candidate through this process on a speculative basis (for my retained clients, I wouldn't take on the project if that was their process) and kept track of the process and the questions asked. Twenty out of the twenty-five interviewers asked basically the same questions, and none of the interviewers had the notes from the previous interviewer (we will come back to this point)

What do you think the candidate thought of the employer's brand after this process? The candidate was offered the role, but he turned them down in favour of another opportunity, which interestingly enough had taken as long to mature (nearly 18 months) where there had been as many stages in the process, but each stage had been unique, provided insight to both the client (yes, it was my client) and the candidate, and every stage had a purpose.

The successful employer, offering basically the same role, with a similar external customer brand had managed to differentiate themselves with their employer brand.

Interviewing

Why don't we train people how to interview? In a manufacturing business if you have a technician who operates a manufacturing robot, do you hire them, give them the manual and then let them get on with it? No, of course, you don't. You induct them; you train them; you supervise them, and then when they are ready, you let them loose on your precious machines.

So why, in people-focused businesses, do firms not train their personnel to interview candidates properly? Sure, they train their HR teams, and they might even circulate suggested interview questions, and, if a manager is really lucky they may get to go on an interview techniques workshop for half a day, but this is the exception and not the rule in my experience.

I think some firms operate with an unhealthy level of assumed knowledge and the attitude that 'Well, surely if this Director or Partner has made it to the top of the firm, then they must know how to interview people just through experience'.

I am sure the Partner is amazing at their job – leading client relationships and solving their issues –but that doesn't mean they are any good at recruiting people. I eat a lot of food, but I am pretty sure I wouldn't make a good Michelin Star chef.

If your business runs on people power (and most do), then your first interaction, your first relationship building opportunity with that new colleague is the interview process. If they feel that the interview was challenging, fair, thorough and interesting, then they will think of you as challenging, fair, thorough and interesting and are likely to be already building a level of respect for you and your organisation before they even walk through the front door.

I have lost count of the number of times I have encountered very senior individuals coming out of meetings saying, 'Well, that was the same meeting as I had last week, just with a different face'. It suggests to individuals that you haven't really thought about the process or briefed your interviewers properly, which in turn suggests that maybe you don't find them important enough to care.

Interview training is readily available. JCM provides, for example, but then so does YouTube and any number of other mediums. If someone has never conducted an interview, then help them, provide them with some training. You wouldn't let them loose on a customer without any training in case they damaged your customer brand, but you are willing to let them damage your employer brand?

I had earlier mentioned interview feedback from previous interviews will be covered, and now I will. See, you didn't have to wait long. If I am the second interviewer of a candidate, I will not conduct the interview until I have either spoken to or seen notes of the previous interview. It's not because I want to form a pre-conceived idea of the person I am interviewing; instead, I want to ask different questions and challenge the individual in a different way for both their and our benefit. For instance, there is no point talking about the candidate's charming but mischievous border collie if the last person already spent 5 minutes doing that in the last interview.

I spend at least thirty minutes preparing for an interview if I am looking to hire someone or am part of the interview team. I will read their CV, read into their character by looking at how they present their CV, check them out on LinkedIn, Google, Hoovers, among others, and from this intelligence, come up with a set of structured questions.

When I interview, I am not looking for answers that are on the CV. Why ask, 'Talk me through your recent career history'? Yawn. What is the point of that? I can read all that from the CV. If anyone ever asks me that question in an interview, I will know they haven't even bothered to read my CV, and I am more than likely to create a completely new one verbally just to see if they will notice. For instance, I want to know why they moved in 1986? What was their motivation to go Fly Fishing in Yemen for a year at the age of 40? What books are they reading? Who they consider to be the key influencers in their life? I also want to know about their perception of our company (because I always have one eye on the employer brand).

Clearly, if it was a technical interview to ascertain the candidate's experience in blockchain technologies, then these questions would be pretty useless, but then I tend to leave the technical interviews to technical colleagues who actually know what they are talking about.

The generational motivators are changing, and no longer can you buy the best talent. This generation – call them anything from Generation Y to the 'Avocado generation' – look for different things from their employers. Sure, they want to be rewarded, but more importantly, they want to be valued and work for a company with values. I have said it before – retention starts at recruitment. Interview properly, interview effectively and value each interaction, and the person you are interviewing will value you.

Feedback

I would say, in my experience, feedback is always the worst performing part of any client's interview process. Ranging from one extreme to the other, if the candidate is good or terrible, extracting feedback from interviews in a form that can then be readily digested by candidates is almost impossible.

I guess it's because it's one of those administrative tasks, like calculating the expenses, and is simply considered a chore to be completed. You've been asked to interview someone on behalf of a colleague, and you don't mind doing that. After all, it's interesting meeting new people, but afterwards, you just want to get on with your day. More importantly, unlike expenses, you won't get anything back afterwards, so the motivation to provide detailed notes following a meeting is limited.

My advice to clients, particularly those with tortuously long interview processes, is not to try and get detailed feedback after each meeting. You are better off getting every interviewer to answer the following four quick questions that can be passed to the next interviewer:
- What is the best thing you liked about the candidate?
- What is the worst thing you didn't like about the candidate?
- What areas of concern do you still have that need to be explored?
- What topics did you ask about?

If you like, provide them with a template, containing gaps between each question, to scribble some notes for the file or email them with the questions straight after the interview (I actually suggest you email them during the interview so that when they get back to their desk or check their phone straight after finishing the interview, those questions are high up in their inbox). Clearly, the sponsor of the hire is going to have to write a much more detailed feedback to be signed off to hire, but they have the motivation to do that because they want to hire.

At the end of the interview process, having hired the candidate, the hiring manager should be provided will all these feedback slips, from which he can then design the development plan for the new hire. By the way, top tip, if you have joined an organisation, and they can't provide you with a personal development plan, then run away (unless you own the company or are the CEO) because you have nothing to learn there. Only ever work for companies that challenge you and where you can learn something every single day. I am forty-five now, and I still can't remember a day when I didn't learn something.

Feedback - The Dark Side

When did you last ask a candidate you didn't offer the job to about how your process? This can be an invaluable source of information for you and often more valid than from those who did secure a role with you. Let's face it, its unlikely people who have just started working for you feel secure enough to criticise the organisations processes.

Systems – Are They Worth It?

Do you run your company on a large double entry book with an accounts clerk meticulously entering sales on a ledger with a quill pen? No, of course, you don't. Systems, when properly selected and implemented, make processes slicker and remove some element of human error.

If you are running a large campaign, with say, 100 candidates, how exactly are you planning to keep track of them, respond to them with feedback in a timely manner, ensure that all meetings are scheduled correctly and more importantly, look after these individuals' personal information in this age of data protection?

You are not going to do this on an excel spreadsheet in the same way that you wouldn't run a multi-million-pound company on a spreadsheet. Applicant Tracking Systems are worth their weight in gold. Although JCM only occasionally runs pure executive search projects these days, we have still invested in the market-leading software to run that part of the business.

Nothing kills an employer brand quicker than interview arrangements going awry, feedback not getting passed on or, more seriously, someone's details being lost or released incorrectly. A properly implemented system should significantly mitigate the considerable risks associated with the process.

These days, with 'software as a service', the cost of such systems is, fortunately, falling rapidly, particularly as they can largely be purchased on a per-seat basis. I will resist the urge to name or recommend a particular supplier, as there is constant innovation in the sector, and any company I name here will be obsolete by the time this book goes to print.

One thing I will say, however, is that in my experience, generalist HR systems (a bit like generalist HR professionals) are not the answer for recruitment and candidate tracking. They may have some functionality, but you are better going for a cheaper system written for the task than bolt on the module of your existing ERP/Management System.

A word on 'Agile TA' and other such systems created by global behemoths – these systems have largely been created by HR teams, not recruitment professionals. All they do is highlight and overcompensate for failed HR processes. Now, if you need to hire thousands of identical technical architects, then it's entirely possible that these systems may present a valid option for you. However, they also extract any sense of personality from the process. They are all about low speed and low-cost mass recruitment. They cannot contribute to your employer branding because you have no real employer branding. Two companies offering the same 'Agile TA' system will appear the same way to the market.

Psychometrics

We often get asked by clients to conduct psychometric evaluations of shortlisted candidates, and they are always somewhat surprised when we explain to them how involved the process actually is. It's not as simple as candidates filling in an online questionnaire and us getting a score out.

I am not a psychologist, and whilst there are some automated online tools out there that produce very pretty-looking reports, I am not a fan. If a client asks for such testing, we always bring in a fully qualified professional who can provide the client with a full range of options.

You see guessing what Myers–Briggs personality type your friends are (I am an ENTJ if you haven't guessed that already) is always a fun quiz down in the pub, but the value of psychometrics doesn't materialise until you have a benchmark. Though there are benchmark industry norms for most job roles that a psychologist may use as a control group, you really want to have already tested people within your organisation for these results to be truly valuable.

A company I have done a lot of work with over the years runs their version of a psychometric test every year as part of their annual appraisal system. They have over 20 years' worth of data of the personality types that exist within their organisational construct and, more importantly, the personality types that are successful.

There is no right or wrong answer to a psychometric test. You are who you are, but a good occupational psychologist will be able to analyse your organisation and provide you with some benchmarks against which you can compare new potential talent.

Chapter 5 – References

Why take references? It's a simple enough question. Why are you taking references? Are you unsure as to the robustness of your own interview process? Do you doubt your colleagues' ability to assess a candidate so much that you think asking the candidates to give you the names of three people who really like them is going to be a game changer? Seriously, who in their right mind is going to give you the names of three people who are going to say anything that isn't glowing about them? These '360' references have been dreamed up in the cauldron of HR and serve no purpose other than to tick a box saying, 'Yes Boss, I have taken up references'.

I am not talking about qualification checks, visa checks, criminal record checks, among others, but about the three people listed at the bottom of the CV as 'references available on request'.

I was once offered a job I didn't want with a large company; the money was great, the role sounded significant, but I just didn't feel a connection throughout the interview process with a number of key stakeholders. They were really keen and nice people, but I struggled to articulate how to say no to the role. Then I thought, 'Simple; they won't hire me if my references are bad'. I couldn't possibly ask any of my friends or colleagues or clients to give me a bad reference, so I hatched a plan and created three people (I also wanted to test my theory on references). They were as follows:
- Bobby Jones – My 'Director' at a previous company;
- Zak Orfman – A previous client; and
- Tony Woolgar – A consultant who used to work for me.

With the wonders of Gmail, Hotmail and Skype, they all had a phone number and email address, and sure enough, each of them was contacted by the head-hunter (yes, even head-hunters use head-hunters).

Bear in mind that the person who made the calls was the same person who had first contacted me about the role, interviewed me, spoke to me after every meeting with feedback (Yes, I know what you are thinking – this head-hunter gives excellent service) and must have had spoken to me at least thirty times in the span of three weeks, and the person at the other end of the phone was me. I had done my best to alter my voice slightly, but let me tell you, John

Culshaw and Rory Bremner have nothing to fear from me. Each call had lasted around ten minutes and covered the same questions as supplied to the head-hunter by the client:

So, all in all, they were not the most glowing of references. Every time one of the referees put up a negative, such as compulsive obsessive behaviour, the head-hunter would try and turn it into a positive, such as 'Ah, so is it fair to say he is obsessed with accuracy and detail then'?

It made not a lot of difference, and I don't know to this day whether the references actually even made it to the client or not. My point, therefore, is that it is a pointless exercise. Now there are going to be some people in my industry spitting their dummies out right about now because they make a good living off of taking references; in fact, some firms even charge extra for it above and beyond their normal fees.

Let me provide a little insider tip right now that would get me kicked out of the magic circle if there was such a thing for headhunters. We love taking references. 'Why?' I hear you ask. Because it provides at least three free business development leads. We get to speak to someone for as long as we like, and we can start building rapport with a potential captive lead while taking the reference. When I worked in a large PLC search environment, if you didn't come away from referencing with a new client meeting, you were considered to have failed. It was the raison d'etre of the whole exercise.

If the candidate has provided the references, then discard them. True 360-degree referencing can be done by higher quality search firms. When I take a reference, I ask the candidate for the three people they suggest, and sure enough, I take those three references (Well I don't want to miss out on a good business development opportunity, do I?), but then the process changes. I then search those three individuals' networks to identify other individuals that I am connected to and that are likely to have known the candidate, and I will keep doing this until I have found enough references to back up and check information that has come out of the interview process. I won't provide names to my client and identify who said what, but I will collate this information and present a summary.

Quality referencing, properly done, can add value to the decision-making process, and it is the reason, I believe, for my proudest statistic from my time as a recruitment professional. It's not the hundreds of searches I have completed, but that no one I placed ever left within the twelve-month guarantee period I always offered my clients.

Chapter 6 – Other Tools and Their Value in Creating your Employer Brand

Every generation of employee looks for different things from their employers, regardless of whether it is the Baby Boomers, Generation X, Y, Millennials (the Avocado generation). Suppose, for argument sake, that you have read, agreed with and implemented every nugget of wisdom in this book, and you now have a world-class, awesome recruitment process that you can be proud of. You know that any potential employee is going to be impressed by your challenging interview questions, comprehensive feedback loops, candidate information, among others. The only problem is that next door to your shiny futuristic HQ building is an almost identical building housing a direct competitor who has also read this book (I believe other books are available, but I can't attest to their quality!).

What next? How else do you make your employer brand stand out? Well, recruitment done well is a process. Employment, however, needs to contain a much wider variety of softer attributes. The good news is that these attributes are tangible; the bad news is they are all hard to implement. Let's tick some of them off, one by one.

Diversity

As I already might have mentioned, I have some friends who can help you with this. Irrespective of your industry, quality potential employees want to work for organisations with no institutional bias around nationality, gender, sexuality, disability and that contain a diverse talent pool. Sure, you might be in a traditional industry that has a historical problem with some of these, but that, in itself, is not the problem. What you are doing about it is the problem and is reflected in the attraction for someone to join.

I once had a client (well, not a client because we didn't accept the work) who approached us and asked us to provide them with some women-only shortlists. I asked them why, and they answered that they had an issue because they had no senior executives who were female. Fair enough, and had they stopped there, I probably would have signed them as a client, but they then went on and blew their foot off with a cruise missile by saying, 'We are going for a public listing on AIM, and we have to be seen to be doing the right thing'. Wrong answer. The sentence alone summed up for me their real attitude to female talent and the corrosive and unhealthy environment that boardroom would be for any female executive to sit in.

If you have an issue, be honest about it, and be honest to candidates about what you are planning or, even better, are actually doing about it.

Corporate Social Responsibility

What self-respecting company these days doesn't have a CSR agenda? The fact you have one is not going to be enough. It has to resonate with both your employees and your customers, and it needs to be meaningful. A headline donation of £10m a year is great but is not so great if it represents less than 1% of your annual profits. In my last business where we had 30+ employees, we offered every individual two days a year for CSR. One day could be given to a charity of their choosing, and one day had to be a company charity that we had collectively chosen. This communicated to people that the company had its own CSR goals, but that it also respected the individuals' own social responsibility goals.

Companies that want to be taken seriously in the CSR arena need to be thinking in terms of 5–10% of profit contribution. Any less, and you are just a part of the crowd.

Eco-Credentials

'Do you use green energy?' 'Are your buildings efficient?' 'Do you recycle?' 'How is your carbon footprint?' 'Do you have a bike or car share scheme?' 'Do you have electric charging points for vehicles in your car park?' These matter to many individuals. Whilst to many people, these are not important considerations, but to enough people, they are. I can think of several candidates I have had on shortlists who have turned down roles because of a company's environmental policies.

Flexibility

We live in an amazing world of technology where we can work seamlessly across continents and hold meetings where we can see each other as if sitting in the same room whilst actually being 2000 miles apart. So, think about this when you are replacing Bob. Did he need to just because he sat at that desk for six years doing that role? Is one-person full time the answer, or would a better answer be two returning to work mothers or fathers who are job-sharing? Some good contacts of mine run a local branch of a franchise recruitment consultancy https://www.ten2two.org/ focussing on the amazing talent that can be found in the returning to work market.

If you can offer flexible working hours, all of a sudden, your available potential talent pool opens wider than everyone else's. Last time I checked, having a baby did nothing to diminish an individual's intellect, capabilities, experience or knowledge. What it did do was that someone might not be as available during the school run times, or that they may only want to work three days a week. I know plenty of people in my own industry that I would take for just one day a week if I could get them.

Other companies that go down the route of employee empowerment offer benefits such as unlimited holidays. DropBox, Github, Workday, Grant Thornton are just a few firms that offer this incentive. What the company is saying to their employees is that 'We trust you; you take the time off you need to be the best employee you can be', which, on an average, results in people actually taking less time off.

Ethics

Depending on the industry, it can be easy to highlight your ethical stance in some situations but harder in others. If you are a bank like the Co-Op that has strict rules as to what type of companies can open accounts with you or an importer of manufactured goods that will only deal with suppliers that meet certain standards of employment conditions in their factory, then you should be able to shout about your ethical practices from the rooftops. If, however, you run a large gambling website, then however 'ethical' you make your product sound, you will remain the devil incarnate to some people. So, what am I saying here? Be honest, be open and be true to whatever you are. Don't try and present yourself as something you are not. In the internet age, any candidate can quickly suss out what is and what isn't the truth.

Fun

Is it fun to work at your company? Does it provide stimulation in addition to what's in your wallet? Do you provide facilities such as onsite or nearby gyms and catering? Do you want to know why successful companies put subsidised coffee franchises in their lobbies? It is not because they like their employees and want to give them cheap coffee; instead they want to keep their employees inside the building so that the employees are around more and end up being more productive for the company.

Google takes it one step further and provides completely free food and drinks at their main campus so that the employees are around from breakfast to dinner. There is a famous story about Brandon, a 23-year-old Google employee from Massachusetts, who actually lives in a truck in the Google car park and saves 90% of his income because he has no living costs. Living on site, every conceivable facility is provided to him from Doctors to Zumba classes.

I am not suggesting that you encourage such behaviour but think about the facilities you provide your employees. If all you have is a chocolate vending machine in your lobby and you work in the middle of an industrial estate, I would suggest you take a good hard look at how you are looking after your people. Simple things, such as decent showers and bike parking for all those who wish to cycle to work, arranging taster sessions for yoga and alternative therapies during lunch breaks, bringing in interesting speakers for seminars, don't have to cost the earth but can have an earth shattering impact on your employer brand.

None of this should even be a surprise to you, as I am not coming down the mountain with carved stone tablets. However, as with most things in life, it's the obvious things we forget.

Pay

I am not going to spend much time on pay, as frankly, it really doesn't affect your employer brand unless you are paying more than 10% differential to the market.

Pay your employees what you yourself would like to be paid for the role they are doing. A good company can split its earnings into 3 pots: 1/3rd for the shareholders, 1/3rd for the staff and 1/3 to invest in the growth of the company.

If you apply the same principle to your employees, they should generally be rewarded with 1/3rd of what they bring to the company, be that in sales and revenue, products or processes.

Personally, I have never had a salary negotiation for myself during the recruitment process. When asked about pay by a potential employer, I have always answered, 'Pay me what you think I am worth', and I have never been disappointed.
If you apply these principles, you won't go far wrong.

The Zany, Wacky and Ridiculous

Now it might come as some surprise to you that I am not a fan of the "wacky races" recruitment practices. If you care to go on Google, or any of your favourite search engines, and type in 'Wacky Recruitment Ideas', you will get pages of listings. What you will notice when reading those, after you have recovered from your sense of disappointment, is that none of them are actually that wacky. I know I was disappointed that not one of the suggestions included a hot air balloon, a lawn mower or a karaoke rendition of Pink!'s latest album.

Why? Because wacky really doesn't work. We are not recruiting clowns for the circus (apologies if you are the HR director for Cirque du Soleil – this probably isn't the book for you); we are recruiting professionals. My exception to this rule is first-time graduates. Do what you like with graduates because a) they love a challenge, and b) anything you have concocted, they have seen coming from a mile away anyway.

By all means, be creative. Not every interview has to be two people looking at each other across a desk, but getting a candidate to do the interview in Morse code by tapping on the wall opposite probably is taking it too far

Chapter 7 – Your HR Department Is Not Your Recruitment Department

One of the big mistakes that companies of all sizes make is misusing their HR department and thinking that they are qualified to lead recruitment activities for the organisation

Now don't get me wrong. I am not devaluing the role of the HR team here at all; I am doing quite the opposite, in fact. HR teams add significant value to any organisation; however, just because recruitment is about people, it doesn't mean it's about HR per se. It's similar, I guess, to the differential between your sales department and your marketing department. Both departments are about getting your product into the market, but both, whilst connected, have different functions.

Of course, many HR personnel have recruitment experience but think about what we are trying to achieve here throughout this book – enhancing your employer brand.

When you order a club sandwich at 2am from a Michelin star restaurant in a five-star hotel, is it the chef who runs the restaurant or a special night chef employed for that task who makes it for you? Both are chefs; both make delicious food, but one is a specialist in one area, and the other is a specialist in another area.

If you want to be the leading employer brand in the marketplace, then the night chef isn't going to cut it – you need the expert, the true specialist who is going to set you apart from every other firm out there.

You are trying to build a following, and people follow what is new or unique or where they perceive the existence of added value.

Now, for a lot of companies, having a full-time recruitment professional sitting around to do occasional appointments would be very wasteful. There, however, are options. An option is to rely on an external recruitment consultancy or search firm. Remember, earlier we spoke about the importance of building a trusted partnership with an external provider. If you have this, then they can become your trusted advisors. Your HR team remains your expert on the technical aspects of the appointment, but your trusted advisors can lead the recruitment process for you.

Another option is to hire an independent specialist. I once ran a 2-year, 27-country campaign for senior executive talent on behalf of a client because they had an HR department but no recruitment expertise. I didn't supply any of the candidates, instead designed and ran the process, managed the external vendors and internal stakeholders and ensured the process ran smoothly.

There are a growing number of recruitment professionals who now operate as independent consultants and will literally work on site 'wearing the company' tie for maybe just one day a month, being the recruitment expert.

The worst mistake that companies make, particularly larger companies, is taking a member of their generalist HR team and making them the Head of Recruitment. In this situation, the best you can hope for, I believe, is a mediocre process that then gets enshrined in company doctrine and becomes the defacto way of doing things. The recruitment machine will work to the Club Sandwich level, and it may be the nicest Club Sandwich you have ever had, but it's not going to win a Michelin star.

Why does it matter? Because you aren't trying to be ordinary; you are trying to be extraordinary and create the best employer brand you possibly can.

Chapter 8 – Ownership

If you are a small business, of say up to 20 people, then you are unlikely to have a full-time recruitment team or HR team, so lay the book down, go make yourself a cup of tea and come back in a minute when everyone has caught up.

Suppose you are a medium to large entity and have not only an HR department but also a recruiter or even a recruitment team. Your ownership talent acquisition is sorted then, isn't it? Well, probably not. I would imagine you think that ownership lies with the Head of HR or the Recruiter? You're wrong. Sure, they can own steps in the process or the mechanics of the process, but they can't own Talent Acquisition. Why is that? Well, it's simple. You or your key stakeholders own your brand and, therefore, also own your employer brand. As the guardian of that brand, you cannot pass off responsibility down to the depths of the organisation; it must remain at a strategic level.

I have met many talented internal recruitment professionals over the years who have been unable to fulfil their true potential to add value to the organisation because the senior stakeholders have taken little interest in the overall process. As a business leader, you must own that process, by all means delegate tasks but ensure that everyone in the organisation knows whose hand is on the tiller.

Often the reason senior leaders give me for not being so involved in the process is that they are too busy with their days jobs. Well, a) that isn't an excuse – remember the previous section on the true costs of recruitment, and b) that just tells me you haven't delegated correctly.

One of the most successful campaigns I ever ran was for a client who had 15 senior requirements across multiple geographies. Rather than hand it down to his country leadership team (who ultimately were going to make the hiring decision), we decided to keep the whole process centralised. This efficiency led to quick processing through the early stages of the process and, ultimately, the strong candidate buying in to the proposition. How much time commitment did that take? About 30 minutes once a week on a call with me. As everyone knew that the regional leader was tracking the progress on a weekly basis, things happened, and the recruitment campaign was prioritised in everyone's to-do lists.

One final point however, if you do hire true Talent Acquisition (not HR) Professionals then Empower them properly. Too often I see recruiters who are powerless to fix a broken process because the "are only a manager". These are your professionals, it doesn't matter if they are lower down the salary scale. When you pop round to your GP you don't tell him how to fix your health just because he is driving a hatchback and you are driving an Aston Martin.

Really good recruitment professionals within an organisation know how to say no, know how to demand the information and feedback they need from the business. If this is not happening in your business then you need to either re-educate your stakeholders or upgrade your team.

Chapter 9 – Good People Are Leaving. Is My Employer Brand Broken?

If you haven't yet created your employer brand, the simple answer is possibly yes. If, however, you have followed the steps above, the answer quite possibly is the opposite.

Let's think about why employees leave an organisation.
- They are unhappy with the organisation;
- There is a lack of progression or career development; and
- You are undervaluing the resource.

Employees can be unhappy with the organisation for a variety of reasons. they might have ethical concerns about the activities of the company; they might disagree with the company's policies or the way it treats people; they might just be bored having worked there for a long time. If you want to listen to your employees, hold regular engagement events with your staff; then you really shouldn't face such issues very often.

If there is a lack of progression or career development, it sounds negative, but it could actually just be the reality. Your company can only grow at the pace your market can accept, and it may be unrealistic to constantly provide greater challenges and better career opportunities for people. If employees are leaving because they are good and need progression, then it should be viewed as a success and celebrated. You should account for the fact that you have developed this individual to the maximum potential you can and now you are celebrating their growth and the fact they are moving on with your blessing. This proactive celebration of someone leaving tells other employers it's all right to grow themselves and develop themselves because they will leave with a lasting favourable view of your organisation, and you never know when you might meet them again!

Chapter 10 – Three Pillars of Creating a Killer Employer Brand

First, you don't need to engage the services of M&C Saatchi to create a killer employer brand. Sure, larger companies trying to reach a larger pool of potential talent can enhance their reach by increasing spending and getting their message to a wider audience, but guess what? If you haven't completed the basic steps that every organisation should, then your message can be flung as far and wide as you like, but it won't make any difference.

Now this book has covered the employer brand topic from several different angles, but it has focussed on the recruitment process. It will come as no surprise to you, therefore, that the first pillar in creating a killer employer brand is:

Getting Your Process Right

The second pillar relates to the fundamentals of the brand itself. You need a very clear definition of what your core values are, what your culture is, what your CSR agenda is, what your attitude to environmental issues or political issues is. I call this:

Getting Your Message Right

The third pillar is how your company operates. Do you offer flexible working hours? Do your offer job share? Is equity available? I call this:

Getting Your Proposition Right

There are whole books written on creating an employer brand, but it's really simple at its core. You are who you are, either celebrate that or change that but don't try and disguise that.

Chapter 11 – Conclusions

Employer brand is a very tenuous concept. It's hard to measure. Sure, you can do polls, and there are plenty of 'Best Companies to Work For' in every imaginable category. That doesn't actually make it any easier to recruit because even if you are number one, it still means there are 10 other organisations close enough to you to make similar claims. Don't mix up 'Best Company to Work for' with employer brand. 'Best Company to work for' is your marketing team's wet dream – better for selling to clients than prospective employees.

Employer brand is subtly different. It's about respect for the individual throughout your business processes, particularly recruitment. It's about doing things significantly differently than the way your competitors do. It's about bucking the perceived wisdom.

I came across a company recently, https://www.hiyacar.co.uk/, which is a peer to peer hire car company. When they are recruiting someone at the offer stage, they offer them a month's salary to walk away from the role rather than accept their offer.

I can't think of a better way to test a potential employee's motivation. The point is, they are doing something that no one else is; therefore, they have become a more attractive employer because they are creating a buzz around their recruitment process. They are creating a unique employer brand.

When Apple launches a new product, it is widely anticipated and pretty much sold out before it even hits the shelves, certainly before the purchaser gets their hands on he device to try it out. There is no reason why your company can't create such anticipation for new roles you create.

Now, you might think that I am only talking about large multinational businesses and their most exciting roles. I'm not. This could be applied to a local business just as easily.

A long-term client of mine leads a telephony and business outsourcing business, Webhelp, which has several large call centre sites around the UK. They have a constant demand to fill what many people might consider mundane 'call centre' roles. These roles are typical first jobs for people whilst they discover what direction they want their careers to take; therefore, there is a quite high turnover of staff through no fault of the company. The only way they can keep recruiting in such high numbers is to the best employer in the area and have the best employer brand they possibly can. This isn't achieved by paying above the market rate; they pay in the upper quartile, but it's still in line with the market standards. They achieve this by offering a fun interesting environment and a professional, slick recruitment process.

Ignore employer brand at your peril. You might not notice the repercussions in the short term. Matters might get trickier in the medium term, but they will become impossible in the long term. At that point, you will be paying above market rates for average talent that has very little emotional investment in your organisation.

If you don't believe what I have said in this book, then ask yourself this. Why does the Walt Disney Company have a Talent Acquisition Marketing department? I would suggest that no one knows branding like Disney knows branding.